Silly Jokes & Amazing Tricks

Christopher & Olivia James

Branson, Missouri, USA

Christopher & Olivia James: Silly Jokes & AmazingnTricks

Printed in the United States of America

ISBN: 978-0-9855789-1-6

Learn more information at: funnyhypermagicboy.com

Dedicated to all of our fans from over the years and everyone that understands the importance of laughter.

Begin your training to become the ultimate Funny Hyper Magic Kid. Hopefully you have the kid thing down. The funny can be found within these pages. The magic will take a bit of practice. The hyper, well, you are on your own with that one. Your studies can be found within these pages as we try to create an army of fun loving, entertaining kids that will soon overtake the world with their jokes, magic, and lively personalities.

This book is perfect for any kid that ever wanted to have the perfect joke, a fun trick, or a puzzling riddle to share with their friends and family. Over the years, I have met millions of audience members from around the world. One thing is universal, people want to be entertained. Now is your chance, go forth, share these jokes, no matter how silly they are, one thing is for sure, you will be remembered.

I've organized this book in the style of my own show. A mixture that will leave you thinking one minute, groaning the next, and laughing a paragraph later. Not every joke is for everyone. However, I feel there is something for everyone.

Enjoy.

Where do ants go for their holidays?

Frants!

What do you call an ant who skips school?

A truant!

What do you get if you cross some ants with some tics?

All sorts of antics!

What medicine would you give an ill ant?

Antibiotics!

What games to ants play with elephants?

Squash!

What do you call a 100 year old ant?

An antique!

What is the biggest ant in the world?

An elephant!

Why don't anteaters get sick?

Because they are full of antibodies!

What do you call an ant who likes to be alone?

An independant!

What kind of ant is good at maths?

An accountant!

What animal do you look like when you get into the bath?

A little bear!

Why do bees hum?

Because they've forgotten the words!

What kind of bees hum and drop things?

A fumble bee!

What do bees do if they want to use public transport?

Wait at a buzz stop!

What do bees chew?

Bumble gum!

What did the bee to the other bee in summer?

Swarm here isn't it!

What is a bee's favorite classical music composer?

Bee-thoven!

Where do bees go on holiday?

Stingapore!

What do you call a bee who's had a spell put on him?

He's bee-witched!

Why do bees buzz?

Because they can't whistle!

Can bees fly in the rain?

Not without their little yellow jackets!

What goes zzub, zzub?

A bee flying backwards!

What are the smartest bees?

Spelling bees!

What bee is good for your health?

Vitamin bee!

Why did the queen bee kick out all of the other bees?

Because they kept droning on and on!

What do you call a bee born in May?

A maybe!

What kind of bee can't be understood?

A mumble bee!

What did the bee say to the naughty bee?

Bee-hive yourself!

Why do bees have sticky hair?

Because of the honey combs!

What do cats eat for breakfast?

Mice Crispies.

Why do cats like to hear other cats make noise?

It's meow-sic to their ears!

Why does everyone love cats?

They're purr-fect!

What do you call a cat who eats lemons?

A sourpuss!

What do you call it when a cat bites?

Catnip!

What's every cat's favorite song?

Three Blind Mice!

What do you call it when a cat stops?

A paws!

What kind of cats lay around the house?

Car-pets!

How do cats buy things?

From a cat-alogue!

What time is it when an elephant sits on the fence?

Time to fix the fence!

What's gray, carries a bunch of flowers and cheers you up when your ill?

A get wellephant!

Policeman: "One of your elephants has been seen chasing a man on a bicycle."

Zoo Keeper: "Nonsense, none of my elephants knows how to ride a bicycle!"

Why do the elephants have short tails?

Because they can't remember long stories!

What's the difference between an African elephant and an Indian elephant?

About 3,000 miles!

Teacher: "Name six wild animals"

Pupil: " Four elephants and two lions!"

What's as big as an elephant but weighs nothing?

An elephant's shadow!

How do you know when there is an elephant under your bed?

When your nose touches the ceiling!

Why were the elephants thrown out of the swimming pool?

Because they couldn't hold their trunks up.

John: I lost my pet dinosaur.

Ron: Why don't you put an ad in the newspaper?

John: What good would that do, she can't read!

What did the Tyrannosaurus rex get after mopping the floor?

Dino-sore!

What do you call a dinosaur that never gives up?

Try-Try-Try-ceratops!

What do you call a dinosaur that smashes everything in its path?

Tyrannosaurus wrecks!

Which dinosaur slept all day?

The dino-snore!

What do you call Tyrannosaurus rex when it wears a cowboy hat and boots?

Tyrannosaurus tex!

What kind of dinosaur can you ride in a rodeo?

A Bronco-saurus!

What's an astronauts favorite drink?

Gravi-tea.

How do you make a baby sleep on a space ship?

You rocket.

What do space cows say?

"Mooooo-n."

What do you call a pan spinning through space?

An unidentified frying object.

What do you call a wizard in space?

A flying saucer-er.

What did the left hand say to the right hand?

How does it feel to always be right?

What did one eye say to the other?

Between me and you, something smells.

Why don't acrobats work in the winter?

They only do Summer-saults.

What do you comb a rabbit with?

A hare brush.

Which rodent won the basketball game?

The porcupine because he had the most points.

What's the difference between a guitar and a fish?

You can't tuna fish.

How do you buy cat food?

Purrr can.

What monkey is always exploding?

A ba-boom.

Why can't you play games in the jungle?

Because there's always gonna be a cheetah.

Three sons left home, went out on their own and prospered.

They discussed the gifts they were able to give their elderly mother.

The first said: "I built a big house for our mother."

The second said: "I sent her a Mercedes with a driver."

The third said: "You remember how our mother enjoys reading the Bible. Now she can't see very well. So I sent her a remarkable parrot that recites the entire Bible. It took elders in the church 12 years to teach him. Mama just has to name the chapter and verse and the parrot recites it."

Soon thereafter, their mother sent out her letters of thanks.

"Milton," she said, "the house you built is so huge. I live only in one room, but I have to clean the whole house.

"Gerald," she said, "I am too old to travel. I stay most of the time at home so I rarely use the Mercedes. And that driver is so rude! He's a pain!"

"But Donald," she said, "the little chicken you sent was delicious!"

Why was the doctor mad?

Because he had no patients!

What is the best time to go to the dentist?

2:30 (tooth hurty)!

What is a polygon?

A dead parrot!

What do you get if you cross a duck with a firework?

A firequaker!

What is a parrot's favorite game?

Hide and Speak!

Why did the parrot wear a raincoat?

Because she wanted to be a Polly unsaturated!

What did the gamekeeper say to the lord of the manor?

'The pheasants are revolting'!

What is the definition of Robin?

A bird who steals!

What do you give a sick bird?

Tweetment!

What's another name for a clever duck?

A wise quacker!

What do you call a crate of ducks?

A box of quackers!

How do you know that owls are cleverer than chickens?

Have you ever heard of Kentucky-fried owl!

How do you get a parrot to talk properly?

Send him to polytechnic!

Where do birds invest their money?

In the stork market!

What do you get if you cross a parrot with a woodpecker?

A bird that talks in morse code!

What birds spend all their time on their knees?

Birds of prey!

What did they call the canary that flew into the pastry dish?

Tweetie Pie!

What kind of birds do you usually find locked up?

Jail-birds!

Why is a sofa like a roast chicken?

Because they're both full of stuffing!

What happens when ducks fly upside down?

They quack up!

What do you get if you cross a woodpecker with a carrier pigeon?

A bird who knocks before delivering its message!

What happened when the owl lost his voice?

He didn't give a hoot!

What do you get if you cross a cat with a bottle of vinegar?

A sourpuss!

What do you get if you cross a cat with a canary?

A peeping tom!

How does a lion greet the other animals in the field?

'Pleased to eat you.'!

What do you get if you cross a tiger with a snowman?

Frostbite!

What is a French cat's favorite pudding?

Chocolate mousse!

What happened when the lion ate the comedian?

He felt funny!

How is cat food sold?

Usually purr can!

What does the lion say to his friends before they go out hunting for food?

'Let us prey.'

What's the unluckiest kind of cat to have?

A catastrophe!

What do you get if you cross a cat with a tree?

A cat-a-logue!

Why was the cat so small?

Because it only ate condensed milk!

What do cows read in the morning?

Moospapers!

Why did the cat frown when she passed the hen house?

Because she heard fowl language!

How is a cat laying down like a coin?

Because he has his head on one side and his tail on the other!

Why did the cat sleep under the car?

Because she wanted to wake up oily!

What did the cat do when he swallowed some cheese?

He waited by the mouse hole with baited breath!

What do you call a lioin who has eaten your mother's sister?

An aunt-eater!

Why did the cat put the letter "M" into the fridge?

Because it turns "ice" into "mice"!

What does a lion brush his mane with?

A catacomb!

What do you get if cross a cat with a canary?

Shredded tweet!

What does a caterpillar do on New Years Day?

Turns over a new leaf!

What pillar doesn't need holding up?

A caterpillar!

Why was the centipede late?

Because he was playing "This little Piggy" with his baby brother!

What do you get if you cross a centipede and a parrot?

A walkie talkie!

What do you get if you cross a centipede and a chicken?

Enough drumsticks to feed an army!

What goes 99-clonk, 99-clonk, 99-clonk?

A centipede with a wooden leg!

Why did the turtle cross the road?

To get to the shell station

Why did the cow cross the road?

To get to the udder side!

Why did the chicken end up in the soup?

Because it ran out of cluck!

What do chickens grow on?

Eggplants!

Why did the chicken cross the basketball court?

He heard the referee calling fowls

Why is it easy for chicks to talk?

Because talk is cheep!

What do you call a rooster who wakes you up at the same time every morning?

An alarm cluck!

What do chicken families do on Saturday afternoon?

They go on peck-nics!

How long do chickens work?

Around the cluck!

Why did the chick disappoint his mother?

He wasn't what he was cracked up to be!

Is chicken soup good for your health?

Not if you're the chicken!

Why did the chicken cross the road, roll in the mud and cross the road again?

Because he was a dirty double-crosser!

Why didn't the chicken skeleton cross the road?

Because he didn't have enough guts!

Why did the chicken cross the playground?

To get to the other slide!

Why did the man put his money in the freezer?

He wanted cold hard cash!

What do you get when you cross a snowman with a vampire?

Frostbite.

How do crazy people go through the forest?

They take the psycho path.

What do prisoners use to call each other?

Cell phones.

What do you get from a pampered cow?

Spoiled milk.

Where do polar bears vote?

The North Poll

Where do snowmen keep their money?

In snow banks.

Why do sea-gulls fly over the sea?

Because if they flew over the bay they would be bagels!

What dog keeps the best time?

A watch dog.

Why did the tomato turn red?

It saw the salad dressing!

What did the grape do when it got stepped on?

It let out a little wine!

How do you make a tissue dance?

Put a little boogey in it!

Where do bees go to the bathroom?

At the BP station!

What did the judge say when the skunk walked in the court room?

Odor in the court.

What did the water say to the boat?

Nothing, it just waved.

Why don't skeletons fight each other?

They don't have the guts.

Knock Knock Jokes

Knock Knock!

Who's there?

Cargo!

Cargo who?

CarGo Beep Beep!

Knock Knock!

Who's there?

Cows.

Cows who?

Cows go moo, not who!

Knock Knock!

Who's there?

Boo.

Boo who?

Don't cry, it's only a joke!

Knock Knock!

Who's there?

Rita.

Rita who?

Rita book, you might learn something!

Knock Knock!

Who's there?

Heaven.

Heaven who?

Heaven you heard enough of these silly Knock Knock jokes?

Knock Knock!

Who's there?

Lettuce.

Lettuce who?

Lettuce in, its cold outside!

Knock Knock!

Who's there?

Anita.

Anita who?

Anita tissue....ah-choo! Too late!

Knock Knock!

Who's there?

Honeycomb.

Honeycomb who?

Honeycomb your hair!

Knock Knock!

Who's there?

Justin.

Justin who?

Justin time for dinner!

Knock Knock!

Who's there?

Canoe.

Canoe who?

Canoe come out to play?

Knock Knock!

Who's there?

Beets.

Beets who?

Beets me!

Knock Knock!

Who's there?

Duey.

Duey who?

Duey have to keep telling Knock Knock jokes.

Why do dogs bury bones in the ground?

Because you can't bury them in trees!

Why did the poor dog chase his own tail?

He was trying to make both ends meet!

What do you get if you cross a sheepdog with a rose?

A collie-flower!

Why do dogs wag their tails?

"Because no one else will do it for them!"

Why didn't the dog speak to his foot?

Because it's not polite to talk back to your paw!

What is the dogs favorite city?

New Yorkie!

What did the cowboy say when the bear ate Lassie?

"Well, doggone!"

How can if you have a stupid dog?

It chases parked cars!

What time is it when an elephant sits on the fence?

Time to fix the fence!

What' s grey with red spots?

An elephant with the measles!

What's big and grey and wears a mask?

The elephantom of the opera!

What do you call an elephant at the North Pole?

Lost!

Why were the elephants thrown out of the swimming pool?

Because they couldn't hold their trunks up!

What do you call an arctic cow?

An eskimoo!

Why does a rooster watch TV?

For hentertainment!

What do you call a crate of ducks?

A box of quackers!

Which fish can perform operations?

A Sturgeon!

What do you call a fish with no eyes?

Fsh!

What lives in the ocean, is grouchy and hates neighbors?

A hermit crab!

What do you get from a bad-tempered shark?

As far away as possible!

Why did the whale cross the road?

To get to the other tide!

What insect runs away from everything?

A flee!

What is the difference between a flea and a wolf?

One prowls on the hairy and the other howls on the prairie!

What to you call a Russian flea?

A Moscow-ito!

What do you get if you cross a rabbit and a flea?

Bugs Bunny!

How do you find where a flea has bitten you?

Start from scratch!

How do fireflies start a race?

Ready steady glow!

What is the difference between a fly and a bird?

A bird can fly but a fly can't bird!

Why is it better to be a grasshopper than a cricket?

Because grasshoppers can play cricket but crickets can't play grasshopper!

What is green and can jump a mile in a minute?

A grasshopper with hiccups!

Where would you put an injured insect?

In an antbulance!

How do you know if you have a tough mosquito?

You slap him and he slaps you back!

What do you get if you cross the Batman with an insect?

The Masked-quito!

What has antlers and sucks blood?

A moose-quito!

What is a mosquito's favorite sport?

Skin-diving!

Why are mosquitos religious?

They prey on you!

What do insects learn at school?

Mothmatics!

What's the biggest moth in the world?

A mammoth!

What's pretty, delicate and carries a sub machine gun?

A killer butterfly!

Why was the moth so unpopular?

He kept picking holes in everything!

What did Tom get when he locked Jerry in the freezer?

Mice cubes!

What mouse was a Roman emperor?

Julius Cheeser!

What do you get if you cross a frog and a dog?

A croaker spaniel!

What does a spider do when he gets angry?

He goes up the wall!

Why are spiders good swimmers?

They have webbed feet!

How do you spot a modern spider?

He doesn't have a web he had a website!

What did the spider say to the fly?

We're getting married do you want to come to the webbing?

Why was the glow worm unhappy?

Because her children weren't that bright!

What reads and lives in an apple?

A bookworm!

What did the woodworm say to the chair?

It's been nice gnawing you!

Why are glow worms good to carry in your bag?

They can lighten your load!

What do you get if you cross a dog with a airplane?

A jet setter!

Where do Eskimos train their dogs?

In the mush room!

Why did the snowman call his dog Frost?

Because frost bites!

Why don't dogs make good dancers?

Because they have two left feet!

What kind of dog does Dracula have?

A bloodhound!

What is the only kind of dog you can eat?

A hot dog!

What's yellow on the outside and grey on the inside?

An elephant disguised as a banana!

What's grey, carries a bunch of flowers and cheers you up when your ill?

A get wellephant!

What' s grey, has four legs and jumps up and down?

An elephant on a trampoline!

What's grey and wrinkly and jumps every twenty seconds?

An elephant with hiccups!

What's as big as an elephant but weighs nothing?

An elephant's shadow!

How do you know when there is an elephant under your bed?

When your nose touches the ceiling!

What did the grape say when the elephant stood on it?

Nothing, it just let out a little wine!

What kind of doctor treats ducks?

A quack!

What did the well mannered sheep say to his friend at the field gate?

After ewe!

Why did the ram fall over the cliff?

He didn't see the ewe turn!

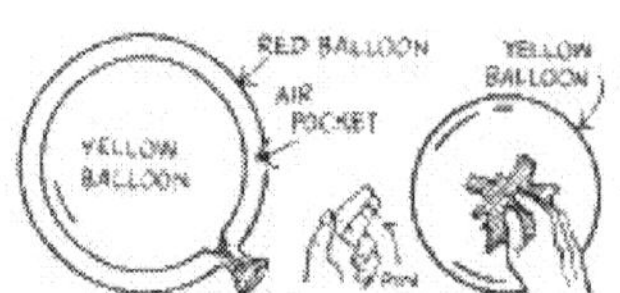

Blooie Balloons

A RED BALLOON IS SHOWN. IN A FLASH, A LOUD REPORT IS HEARD, AND THE RED BALLOON CHANGES TO YELLOW!

PREPARE THIS TRICK BY STUFFING A YELLOW BALLOON INSIDE A RED ONE. BLOW UP THE INNER YELLOW BALLOON, THE RED ONE WILL SWELL UP WITH IT. TIE THE NECK OF THE YELLOW BALLOON WITH A RUBBER BAND. NOW BLOW MORE AIR INTO THE RED ONE TO CAUSE AN AIR POCKET BETWEEN THE BALLOONS. HOLDING THE RED BALLOON ALOFT, PRICK IT WITH A SECRETLY HELD PIN. THE RED ONE WILL BURST AND THE YELLOW BALLOON REMAINS!

What do cows like to dance to?

Any kind of moosic you like!

Where do sheep get shaved?

At the baa baas!

What do you give a pony with a cold?

Cough Stirrup!

What is a horse's favorite sport?

Stable tennis!

What did the farmer call the cow that would not give him any milk?

An udder failure!

What do you give a sick pig?

Oinkment!

What is a pigs favorite ballet?

Swine Lake!

What do you get if you cross a hen with a dog?

Pooched eggs!

Why did the pony cough?

Because he was a little horse!

What is the opposite of cock-a doodle-doo?

Cock-a-doodle-don't!

Where do milkshakes come from?

Excited cows!

Where do shellfish go to borrow money?

To the prawn broker!

What happened to the shark who swallowed a bunch of keys?

He got lockjaw!

Where do fish wash?

In a river basin!

What fish only swims at night?

A starfish!

Which fish go to heaven when they die?

Angelfish!

What is the best way to communicate with a fish?

Drop it a line!

What kind of horse can swim underwater without coming up for air?

A seahorse!

Where do frogs keep their money?

In a river bank!

What kind of bull doesn't have horns?

A bullfrog!

What jumps up and down in front of a car?

Froglights!

Why was the frog down in the mouth?

He was un hoppy!

Whats green and can jump a mile a minute?

A frog with hiccups!

Why did the lizard go on a diet?

It weighed too much for its scales!

What do toads drink?

Croaka-cola!

What do you get if cross a science fiction film with a toad?

Star Warts!

What kind of shoes to frogs like?

Open toad sandals!

What goes up and down but does not move?

Stairs

Where should a 500 pound alien go?

On a diet

What did one toilet say to the other?

You look a bit flushed.

Why did the picture go to jail?

Because it was framed.

What did one wall say to the other wall?

I'll meet you at the corner.

What did the paper say to the pencil?

Write on!

What do you call a boy named Lee that no one talks to?

Lonely

What gets wetter the more it dries?

A towel.

Why do bicycles fall over?

Because they are two-tired!

Why do dragons sleep during the day?

So they can fight knights!

What did Cinderella say when her photos did not show up?

Someday my prints will come!

Why was the broom late?

It over swept!

What part of the car is the laziest?

The wheels, because they are always tired!

What did the stamp say to the envelope?

Stick with me and we will go places!

We're you long in the hospital?

No, I was the same size I am now!

Why couldn't the pirate play cards?

Because he was sitting on the deck!

What did one elevator say to the other elevator?

I think I'm coming down with something!

Why was the belt arrested?

Because it held up some pants!

Why was everyone so tired on April 1st?

They had just finished a March of 31 days.

Why can't your nose be 12 inches long?

Because then it would be a foot!

What makes the calendar seem so popular?

Because it has a lot of dates!

What is it that even the most careful person overlooks?

Her nose!

Did you hear about the robbery last night?

Two clothes pins held up a pair of pants!

Why do you go to bed every night?

Because the bed won't come to you!

Why did Billy go out with a prune?

Because he couldn't find a date!

Why do eskimos do their laundry in Tide?

Because it's too cold out-tide!

What has four wheels and flies?

A garbage truck!

What kind of car does Mickey Mouse's wife drive?

A minnie van!

Why don't traffic lights ever go swimming?

Because they take too long to change!

Why did the man run around his bed?

To catch up on his sleep!

Why did the robber take a bath before he stole from the bank?

He wanted to make a clean get away!

Why did the policeman go to the baseball game?

She heard someone had stolen a base!

Why did the book join the police?

He wanted to go undercover!

Why was there thunder and lightning in the lab?

The scientists were brainstorming!

What do lawyers wear to court?

Lawsuits!

What did the lawyer name his daughter?

Sue

What kind of card does a farmer drive?

A cornvertable!

What do you call a flying police officer?

A helicopper!

How did the farmer mend his pants?

With cabbage patches!

Why did the lazy man want a job in a bakery?

So he could loaf around!

Why did the farmer ride his horse to town?

It was too heavy to carry!

What do you call a happy cowboy?

A jolly rancher.

When does a doctor get mad?

When he runs out of patients!

Why did the pillow go to the doctor?

He was feeling all stuffed up!

Bloody Puzzler

ASK SOMEONE TO HOLD A RULER IN ONE HAND, AND A PENCIL IN THE OTHER. AS YOUR BACK IS TURNED, REQUEST THAT HE HOLD JUST ONE OF THE OBJECTS HIGH OVER HIS HEAD. AFTER A FEW MINUTES, TELL HIM TO PLACE BOTH OBJECTS ON THE TABLE, STILL HOLDING THEM.

TURNING AROUND, YOU NOW TELL HIM WHICH OBJECT HE HELD ALOFT!

THE SECRET IS IN THE PERSON'S HANDS. THE HAND THAT WAS RAISED WILL BE PALER THAN THE OTHER AND THE VEINS SMALLER DUE TO THE BLOOD LEAVING IT AS IT WAS RAISED!

What did on tonsil say to the other tonsil?

Get dressed up, the doctor is taking us out!

Did you hear the one about the germ?

Never mind, I don't want to spread it around

Where does a boat go when it's sick?

To the dock!

Why did the cookie go to the hospital?

He was feeling really crumbie!

What did the judge say to the dentist?

Do you swear to pull the tooth, the whole tooth and nothing but the tooth?

Why did the tree go to the dentist?

To get a root canal.

Why did the king go to the dentist?

To get his teeth crowned!

What time do you go to the dentist?

Tooth-Hurty!

What does a dentist do during an earthquake?

She braces herself!

What did the tooth say to the dentist as she was leaving?

Fill me in when you get back

What is a dentist's favorite animal?

A molar bear!

What did the dentist get for an award?

A little plaque

What has one head, one foot and four legs?

A Bed

Did you hear the joke about the roof?

Never mind, it's over your head!

How many letters are in The Alphabet?

There are 11 letters in The Alphabet

How can you spell cold with two letters?

IC (icy)

If you were in a race and passed the person in 2nd place, what place would you be in?

2nd place!

What is the center of gravity?

The letter V!

What has a head, a tail, is brown, and has no legs?

A penny!

What goes up, but never comes down?

Your age!

What gets bigger and bigger as you take more away from it?

A hole!

How many months have 28 days?

All of them!

How many books can you put into an empty backpack?

One! After that it's not empty.

Which weighs more, a ton of feathers or a ton of bricks?

Neither, they both weigh a ton!

Does your shirt have holes in it?

No, then how did you put it on?

What starts with a P and ends with an E and has a million letters in it?

Post Office!

When does a cart come before a horse?

In the dictionary!

What is full of holes but can still hold water?

A sponge!

What has two hands, a round face, always runs, but stays in place?

A clock!

Where does success come before work?

In the dictionary!

What breaks when you say it?

Silence!

What did the ground say to the earthquake?

You crack me up!

Why did the music teacher need a ladder?

To reach the high notes.

Why did nose not want to go to school?

He was tired of getting picked on!

How do you get straight A's?

By using a ruler!

Why did the kid study in the airplane?

Because he wanted a higher education!

How did the music teacher get locked in the classroom?

His keys were inside the piano!

What do elves learn in school?

The elf-abet!

What object is king of the classroom?

The ruler!

How does the barber cut the moon's hair?

E-clipse it!

What happened when the wheel was invented?

It caused a revolution!

What do librarians take with them when they go fishing?

Bookworms

What is the world's tallest building?

The library because it has the most stories.

What vegetables to librarians like?

Quiet peas.

Why did the clock in the cafeteria run slow?

It always went back four seconds.

Why didn't the sun go to college?

Because it already had a million degrees!

Why were the early days of history called the dark ages?

Because there were so many knights!

Why is England the wettest country?

Because the queen has reigned there for years!

How did the Vikings send secret messages?

By norse code!

What kind of lighting did Noah use for the ark?

Floodlights!

What did Mason say to Dixon?

We've got to draw the line here!

Who made King Arthur's round table?

Sir-Cumference

Who built the ark?

I have Noah idea!

Where was the Declaration of Independence signed?

At the bottom!

What is the fruitiest subject at school?

History, because it's full of dates!

When a knight was killed in battle, what sign did they put on his grave?

Rust in peace!

How was the Roman Empire cut in half?

With a pair of Caesars!

Why didn't the quarter roll down the hill with the nickel?

Because it had more cents.

Why was the math book sad?

Because it had too many problems.

What kind of meals do math teachers eat?

Square meals!

Why didn't the two 4's want any dinner?

Because they already 8!

What is a math teacher's favorite sum?

Summer!

What do you get when you divide the circumference of a Jack-o-lantern by its diameter?

Pumpkin Pi!

What did zero say to the number eight?

Nice belt.

Why did the teacher wear sunglasses?

Because his class was so bright!

Why were the teacher's eyes crossed?

She couldn't control her pupils!

Teacher: You missed school yesterday, didn't you?

Student: Not really.

Teacher: If I had 6 oranges in one hand and 7 apples in the other, what would I have?

Student: Big hands!

Teacher: If you got $20 from 5 people, what you get?

Student: A new bike.

Teacher: I hope I didn't see you looking at John's exam?

Student: I hope you didn't either.

Teacher: What is the shortest month?

Student: May, it only has three letters.

Why did the teacher turn the lights on?

Because her class was so dim.

Where do the pianists go for vacation?

Florida Keys

What is the smartest state?

Alabama, it has four A's and one B.

Where to pencils come from?

Pennsylvania!

Teacher: Where is the English Channel?

Student: I don't know, my TV doesn't pick it up!

What is the capital of Alaska?

Come on, Juneau this one!

What rock group has four men that don't sing?

Mount Rushmore!

What city cheats at exams?

Peking!

What is the capital of Washington?

The W!

What did Delaware?

Her New Jersey!

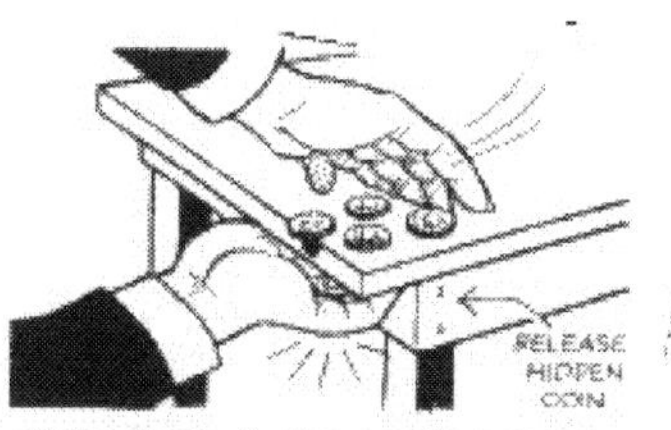

Multiplying Coins

YOU PLACE 4 COINS ON THE TABLE. YOU NOW TELL YOUR FRIENDS THAT YOU CAN, WITH YOUR MYSTERIOUS POWERS, CAUSE THE 4 COINS TO CONVERT INTO 5! SECRETLY, YOU HAVE ATTACHED A COIN (WITH A DAB OF SOAP) TO THE UNDERSIDE OF THE TABLE. BRUSH THE COINS INTO YOUR CUPPED LEFT HAND AND AT THE SAME TIME RELEASE THE HIDDEN COIN. IMMEDIATELY MAKE A FIST AROUND THE COINS. ASK SOMEONE TO TOUCH YOUR FIST, THEN OPEN YOUR HAND, AND BEHOLD.... *THERE ARE FIVE COINS!*

What is the fastest country in the world?

Rush-a!

Teacher: What can you tell me about the Dead Sea?

Student: I didn't even know it was sick!

How can you tell the ocean is friendly?

It waves.

What kind of hair do oceans have?

Wavy!

What did Mars say to Saturn?

Give me a ring sometime.

What did the big flower say to the small flower?

What's up Bud.

Where does seaweed go to look for a job?

The kelp wanted section.

When is the moon the heaviest?

When it's full!

What type of songs do the planets sing?

Nep-tunes!

What kind of flower grows on your face?

Tulips!

What washes up on very small beaches?

Microwaves!

What do you call an attractive volcano?

Lava-ble!

What did the tornado say to the sports car?

Want to go for a spin!

What kind of shorts to clouds wear?

Thunderwear!

What's a tornado's favorite game?

Twister!

What did one volcano say to the other volcano?

I lava you!

What bow can't be tied?

A rainbow!

What falls but never hits the ground?

The temperature!

What happens when the fog disperses in California?

UCLA!

What did the tree wear to the pool party?

Swimming trunks!

What did the beaver say to the tree?

It's been nice gnawing you!

What is a tree's least favorite month?

Sep-timber!

What kind of tree can fit into your hand?

A palm tree!

How do trees get on the internet?

They log in.

How can you tell that a tree is a dogwood tree?

By its bark!

What did the little tree say to the big tree?

Leaf me alone!

Why did the pine tree get into trouble?

Because it was being knotty

What did the tree do when the bank closed?

It started a new branch

What do you call cheese that isn't yours?

Nacho cheese!

Why do the French like to eat snails?

Because they don't like fast food!

Why did the fisherman put peanut butter into the sea?

To go with the jellyfish!

Why shouldn't you tell an egg a joke?

Because it might crack up!

What did the baby corn say to it's mom?

Where is pop corn?

What kind of nuts always seems to have a cold?

Cashews!

Waiter, will my pizza be long?

No sir, it will be round!

What is green and sings?

Elvis Parsley

Why did the banana go to the doctor?

Because it wasn't peeling well!

What candy do you eat on the playground?

Recess pieces.

Why don't you starve in a desert?

Because of all the 'sand which is' there.

How do you make a walnut laugh?

Crack it up!

In which school do you learn to make ice cream?

Sunday School.

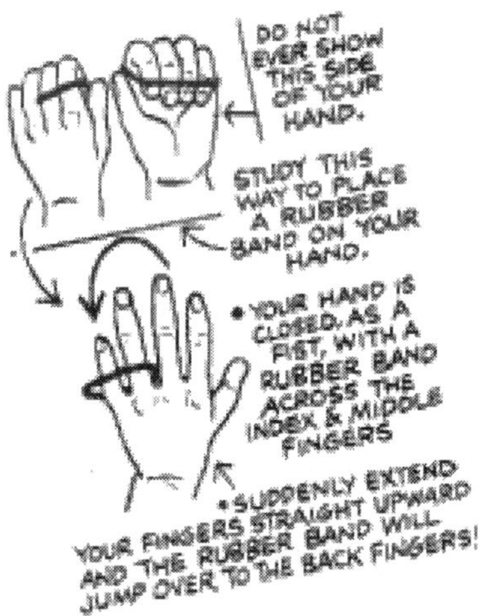

What do elves make sandwiches with?

Shortbread

Why shouldn't you tell a secret on a farm?

Because the potatoes have eyes and the corn has ears.

What is a pretzel's favorite dance?

The Twist!

What are twins favorite fruit?

Pears!

If a crocodile makes shoes, what does a banana make?

Slippers!

What do you give to a sick lemon?

Lemon aid!

Why did the lady love to drink hot chocolate?

Because she was a cocoanut!

How do you make a milk shake?

Give it a good scare!

What do you call a peanut in a spacesuit?

An astronut!

What kind of keys to kids like to carry?

Cookies!

Why don't they serve chocolate in prison?

Because it makes you break out!

What is a cow's favorite day?

Moo-years Day!

What do you get when you plant kisses?

Two lips.

Where does the Easter bunny get his breakfast?

IHOP!

How does the Easter bunny stay in shape?

Lots of eggercise!

What was the most popular dance in 1776?

Indepen-dance!

What do you call a fake stone in Ireland?

A sham rock

Why does Santa Claus like to go down the chimney?

Because it soots him!

What do Santa's elves do after school?

Their gnomework!

What do snowmen like to eat for breakfast?

Frosted Flakes!

What is a parent's favorite Christmas carol?

Silent Night.

What is the fear of Santa Claus called?

Claustrophobia

What nationality is Santa Claus?

North Polish!

Why does Santa have a garden?

So he can hoe, hoe, hoe!

Why did the dog hand up his stocking at Christmas?

He was waiting for Santa Paws.

Why is it cold on Christmas?

Because it's in Decembrrrrrrrr!

What happened when the turkey got into a fight?

He got the stuffing knocked out of him!

Who isn't hungry on Thanksgiving?

The turkey, because he's already stuffed!

Who was the drummer in the Thanksgiving band?

The turkey, because he had the drumsticks!

What do you call a single vampire?

A bat-chelor.

Why didn't the skeleton cross the road?

He didn't have the guts!

Why are graveyards noisy?

Because of all the coffin!

What is a scarecrows favorite fruit?

Straw-berries!

What did the boy ghost say to the girl ghost?

You sure are Boo-tiful!

Why was the baby ghost sad?

He wanted his mummy!

What do witches put on their bagels?

Scream Cheese

What did the vampire say about the Dracula movie?

It was fang-tastic!

Why are vampires tough to get along with?

Because they can be pains in the neck!

Do you know how to make a witch itch?

You take away the w!

What subject in school is easy for a witch?

Spell-ing

What do you call a cow that won't give milk?

A milk dud!

When is a well dressed lion like a weed?

When he's a dandelion (dandy lion)

What do you call a sleeping bull?

A bull-dozer.

Why do gorillas have big nostrils?

Because they have big fingers!

Why are teddy bears never hungry?

They are always stuffed!

Why are fish so smart?

Because they live in schools.

What happened when the lion ate the comedian?

He felt funny!

What fish only swims at night?

A starfish!

Why is a fish easy to weigh?

Because it has its own scales!

Why did the lion spit out the clown?

Because he tasted funny!

What do you get when you cross a snake and a pie?

A pie-thon!

What did the buffalo say to his son when he went away on a trip?

Bison!

Why didn't the boy believe the tiger?

He thought it was a lion!

How do bees get to school?

By school buzz!

What do you call a bear with no ears?

B!

What animal has more lives than a cat?

Frogs, they croak every night!

What do you call a dinosaur with no eyes?

Doyouthinkysaraus

What do you call a sleeping dinosaur?

A dino-snore!

What dinosaur would Harry Potter be?

The Dinosorcerer

Why was the Stegosaurus such a good volleyball player?

Because he could really spike the ball!

What does a triceratops sit on?

Its tricera-bottom.

What do dinosaurs use on the floors of their kitchens?

Rep-tiles

What's the nickname for someone who put their right hand in the mouth of a T-Rex?

Lefty

What do you call a paleontologist who sleeps all the time?

Lazy bones

What do you get when a dinosaur scores a touchdown?

A dino-score

What did the dinosaur use to build his house?

A dino-saw

What do you call four bullfighters in quicksand?

Quattro sinko.

What do you call a boomerang that doesn't work?

A stick.

What is a ghosts favorite position in soccer?

Ghoul keeper.

What is a Cheerleader's favorite food?

Cheerios!

Why can't Cinderella play soccer?

Because she's always running away from the ball.

When is a baby good at basketball?

When it's dribbling!

Why did the basketball player go to jail?

Because he shot the ball.

Why do basketball players love donuts?

Because they dunk them!

What do you call a pig who plays basketball?

A ball hog!

Why did the golfer wear two pairs of pants?

In case he got a hole in one!

How is a baseball team similar to a pancake?

They both need a good batter!

What's a golfer's favorite letter?

Tee!

What animal is best at hitting a baseball?

A bat!

At what sport to waiters do really well?

Tennis, because they can serve so well.

How do baseball players stay cool?

They sit next to the fans.

Why did the football coach go to the bank?

He wanted his quarter back!

What is harder to catch the faster you run?

Your breath!

Why is tennis such a loud sport?

The players raise a racquet.

Why did the ballerina quit?

Because it was tu-tu hard!

What is an insects favorite sport?

Cricket!

What is the hardest part about skydiving?

The ground!

What did the spider do on the computer?

Made a website!

What did the computer do at lunchtime?

Had a byte!

What does a baby computer call his father?

Data!

Why did the computer keep sneezing?

It had a virus!

What is a computer virus?

A terminal illness!

Why was the computer cold?

It left it's Windows open!

What do you get when you cross a computer and a life guard?

A screensaver!

Where do all the cool mice live?

In their mousepads

Why don't aliens eat clowns.

Because they taste funny.

What do you call a fish with no eyes?

A fsh

How do you make a goldfish age?

Take out the "g"

What's the richest kind of air?

Billionaire.

What do skeletons say before a meal?

Bone appetite.

Why did the Skeleton go to the movies by himself?

He had no body to go with him.

What do you call a cow with a twitch?

Beef jerky.

Where do very smart hot dogs end up?

On honor rolls.

Why did the mother cat move her kittens?

She didn't want to litter.

What do you get when you cross a pig and a cactus?

A porky-pine.

What's at the bottom of the ocean and shakes?

A nervous wreck.

What did the mountain climber name his son?

Cliff.

Which runs faster, hot or cold?

Hot. Everyone can catch cold.

Why is it so hot in a stadium after a football game?

Because all the fans have left.

Why is a lost Dalmatian easily found?

Because he's always spotted.

Why was six afraid of seven?

Because seven eight nine!

What has ten letters and starts with gas?

An automobile.

Three guys, stranded on a desert island, find a magic lantern containing a genie. The genie grants them each one wish. The first guy wishes he was off the island and back home -- and poof!, he is back home. The second guy wishes the same thing -- and poof!, he is gone too. The third guy says, "I'm lonely. I wish my friends were back here."

What do you call an alligator in a vest?

An investigator!

When do kangaroos celebrate their birthdays?

On a leap year!!

What do you call a snail on a ship?

A snailer!

What do you get when you throw all the books in the world in the ocean?

A title wave

Where do cows go on a Saturday night?

To the mooooovies

what day do potatos hate the most?

fry-day!

Why can't jungle animals take a test?

Too many cheetahs!

Peculiar Paper Tear

YOU SHOW A 4"x4" SQUARE OF TISSUE PAPER. PROCEDE TO TEAR IT INTO SMALL PIECES. NOW ROLL UP THE TORN PIECES INTO A BALL, SQUEEZING IT AS YOU DO SO. WITH A SHOUT OF "PRESTO", UNROLL THE BALL AND THE PIECE OF PAPER IS WHOLE & RESTORED!

BEFORE PRESENTING THIS TRICK, ROLL A DUPLICATE 4"x4" TISSUE INTO A BALL, AND HIDE IT IN YOUR HAND. WHEN DOING THIS STUNT, SIMPLY TRADE PLACES WITH THE TORN PIECES AND THE WHOLE PIECES, WHILE YOU ARE GOING THRU THE SQUEEZING MOTION.

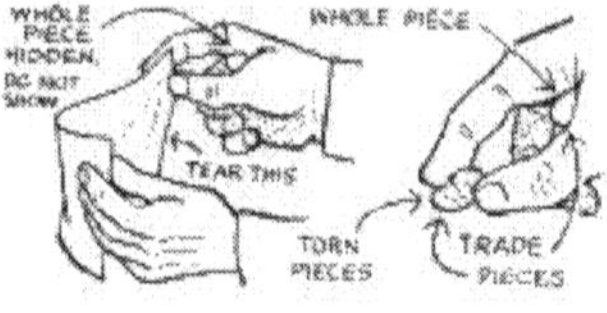

What kind of room can you eat?

A mushroom!

Which side of a parrot has the most feathers?

The outside!

April showers bring mayflowers, then what do mayflowers bring?

Pilgrims!!!

What is orange and sounds like a parrot?

A carrot.

What did the man who lost his left side say?

Im all right now!

What is the difference between Bird Flu and Swine Flu?

For bird flu you need tweetment and for swine flu you need oinkment.

What is the longest word?

Smiles; because it has a mile in between.

What comes after a monkey?

It's tail.

What goes up when the rain comes down?

An Umbrella.

Why did the skeleton go to the barbeque?

Because he wanted some spare ribs.

What is the difference between a unicorn and a lettuce?

One is a funny beast, and the other is a bunny feast.

What did one magnet say to the other magnet?

I find you very attractive.

What's big, grey and goes round and round?

An elephant stuck in a revolving door.

What's worse than finding a worm in your apple?

Finding half a worm.

How do you stop a dog from smelling?

Block his nose.

What did the snail say when he got a ride on a turtle?

"Wheeeeeeeeeeeeeeeee!"

What do you call an annoying vampire?

A pain in the neck.

What do sea monsters eat?

Fish and ships.

Where did the spaghetti go to dance?

The meat ball!

What always falls but never gets hurt?

Rain!

How do you know that carrots are good for your eyes?

Ever seen a rabbit wearing glasses?

What has four legs but can't run?

A table!

What has no beginning, no end and nothing in the middle?

A doughnut!

What do you call a cow that just had a calf?

De-CALF-enated!

What are two things you can't have for lunch?

Breakfast and dinner!

Why did the computer need glasses?

To fix his web sight.

I run but I never walk. I have a mouth but never eat. I have a bed but never sleep. What am I?

A river

Why did the young cat get arrested ?

For his litter!

Why are rivers so rich?

Because they have 2 banks.

Why didn't the skeleton go to the school dance?

He had no body to go with.

What gets wet the more it dries?

A towel!

What is a TV's favorite thing to do at the the beach?

Channel surf.

Why were the police suspicious of the window blinds?

They were shady.

Why did the baker go to jail?

Because he got caught beating the eggs.

The person who makes it sells it, the person who buys it never uses it and the person who is using it never knows they're using it. What is it?

A coffin.

What did the math book say to the other math book?

I have problems!

What do you do when your fish sings flat?

Tuna fish!

What can you catch but not throw?

A cold.

Why did the pelican get kicked out of the restaurant?

Because he had a big bill.

Which wolf got lost in the woods?

The wherewolf.

What do you call a cow with no legs?

Ground beef!

What does a train say that a teacher says not to do?

A teacher says, "Spit out your gum," while a train says, "Choo choo!"

What color is a burp?

BURPle!

What's a monster's favourite game?

Swallow the Leader!

What do you get when you cross a hammock and a dog?

A rocker spaniel.

Why did the nose feel sad?

Because he always got picked on!

Why was Cinderella kicked off the football team?

She ran away from the ball!

What do you call a cat that ate a lemon?

A sourpuss.

How do trees get online?

They log on!

What is a cat's favorite color?

PURRple.

What did one chair say to the other?

"What are you sitting around for?"

I'm at the beginning of eternity and the end of time and space. I'm at the beginning of every end and the end of every place. What am I?

The letter E!

What has lots of teeth but can't chew a thing?

A comb!

What is so fragile that it breaks when you say it?

Silence!

Why did the banana got to the doctor?

Because he wasn't peeling very well.

Why did the orange stop rolling?

It ran out of juice!

What's it called when a snowman has a temper tantrum?

A meltdown!

Why was the broom late for school.

He over swept.

Which country is the slipperiest?

Greece!

Appendix A: Abra-KID-abra Activity Book

Years ago, I toured doing my motivational kid's show for elementary schools. I called it the "Kids First" show. I met thousands of kids and to this day, still have some that contact me on a regular basis. Following, is my kids activity book that I gave out to the children I was lucky enough to meet.

Adding these pages to this book, have brought back so many memories of interesting shows, laughing children, and the wonderful people that made me what I am today. I learned so much about being a real performer during those years. I learned how to deal with any unforseen circumstances and less than ideal performance situations. Most of all, I learned how to perform for every walk of life and age. How to keep the administrators and teachers laughing as much as the children, and how to make them want to have you back again.

I hope you share these with a young person you know and enjoy the sense of wonder I witnessed from those stages so many years ago.

Abra-KID-abra!
WELCOME!

Welcome tothe wonderful world of magic, fun and excitement!

This is your **"Abra-KID-abra"** Magic, Coloring, And Activity Fun Book. In it you will find all sorts of exciting and fun tricks, activities and adventures to enjoy.

Magic is thousands of years old. Ancient secrets of some of the world's best magicians are told here. Enjoy having fun with your friends while showing them some of the amazing tricks you'll learn in the pages of this book. Remember part of the power and mystique of magic is in the **secrets**!

- ☐ The first rule of magic is **NEVER tell how the trick is done!**
- ☐ The second rule of magic is **never do the same trick twice for the same audience!**
- ☐ The third rule of magic, which really "should be" the very **first** rule of magic, is to **always practice your magic before you show it to anybody.** We have purposefully selected simple magic tricks that have high impact and are guaranteed to amaze your friends and family!

Please enjoy all there is to do and learn with your very own ***"Abra-KID-abra!"*** *Magic, Coloring and Activity Fun Book!*

Magically,

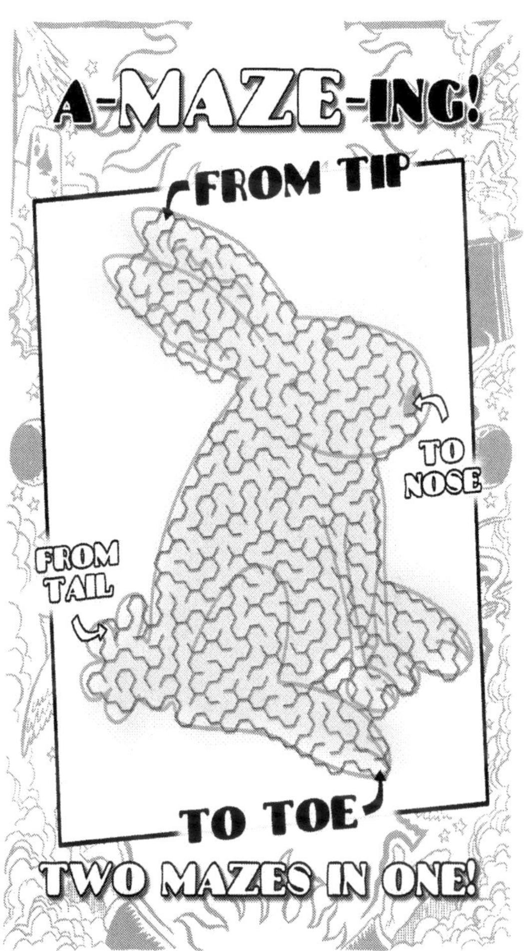
A-MAZE-ING!
FROM TIP
TO NOSE
FROM TAIL
TO TOE
TWO MAZES IN ONE!

the
APPEARING
GIRL!
Help Her Find Her Way
To The Big Show!
Christopher
interactive comedy
POOF!

Funny Stuff:

What kind of cat shouldn't you play cards with?
A Cheetah!

What do Porcupines say to each other when they shake hands?
"Ouch!"

How do you make an elephant float?
Add an elephant to 2 scoops of vanilla ice cream & some milk!

How do you know that carrots are good for your eyesight?
Have you ever seen a rabbit wearing glasses?

What has no beginning, no end, and nothing in the middle?
A doughnut!

Christopher
interactive comedy
The MAGIC Rings!

WOW!
MAGIC

MAGIC YOU CAN DO

COLOR SENSE

What the Audience Sees: You amazingly identify the color of a crayon handed to you behind your back only by touching it.

Super-Secret Tricky Method: Ask someone to take any crayon from a box and hand it to you behind your back. Make sure you don't see it! You then turn to face the audience but keep the crayon behind your back. Secretly dig your right thumb-nail into the crayon wax. Keep hold of the crayon behind your back as you bring your right hand up to your forehead as if concentrating. Take a quick peek at your thumbnail and you will see bits of crayon in it and will know the chosen color. Fake concentrating some more and then dramatically announce the color!

FROM NOT TO KNOT

Effect: A knot mysteriously appears in the corner of a handkerchief.

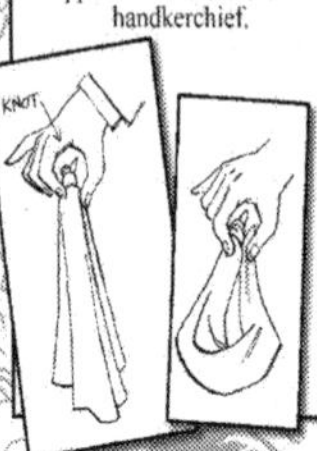

Secret: Before your performance, secretly tie a knot in one corner of a handkerchief. Show the handkerchief but hold it with the knot hidden in your right hand. The left hand now lifts the bottom end of the handkerchief and places it in the right hand along with the top corner. Give the handkerchief a shake and drop the unknotted end. Repeat this three times. On the third attempt allow the knotted corner to drop, retaining your grip on the other corner. All you have done is change the corner you are holding but it appears that the knot has formed by magic.

COOL MAGIC TRICKS

JUMPING BAND

Put a rubber band around your first and second fingersso that it looks like figure1 from the front. As you stretch the rubber band, secretly put all your fingertips inside the band. This is not seen by the audience.

Tell them the rubber band will amazingly jump across to the other two fingers. All you need to do is straighten out your fingers, and the band will move to the other fingers as in figure 3.

1

2

3

ELBOW Grease

Show everyone a single coin. Tell all that by rubbing your elbow with it, you can change it into two coins! And you do it!

Before doing this trick hide a similar coin in your collar (fig.1) as you rub your elbow, grasp the hidden coin and, as you bring your hands together, you can show your audience two coins where there was once just one!!!

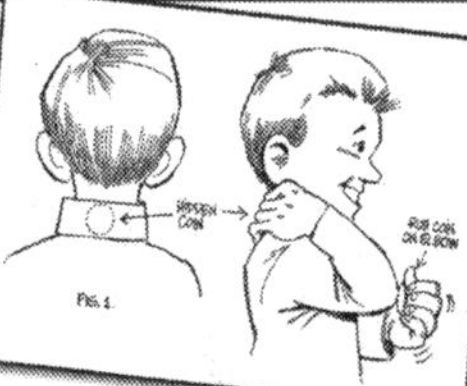

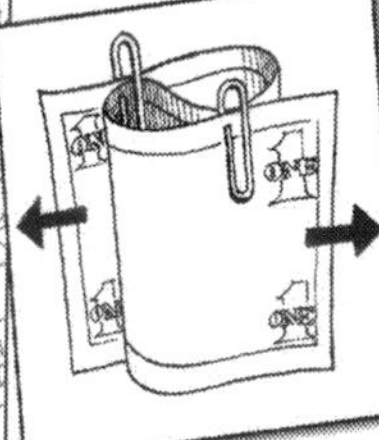

Acrobatic Clips!

Fold a dollar bill in an 'S' shape, and attach two paperclips as shown below. Tell everybody that the paperclips will be launched into the air, and in the middle of thier acrobatic flight, will come together and impossibly link... right in mid-air!

With a drumroll, pull the two ends of the bill sharply in opposite directions. The clips will come together and jump into the air all by themselves. Now you just need to catch the paperclips, show them linked together, and take your bow!

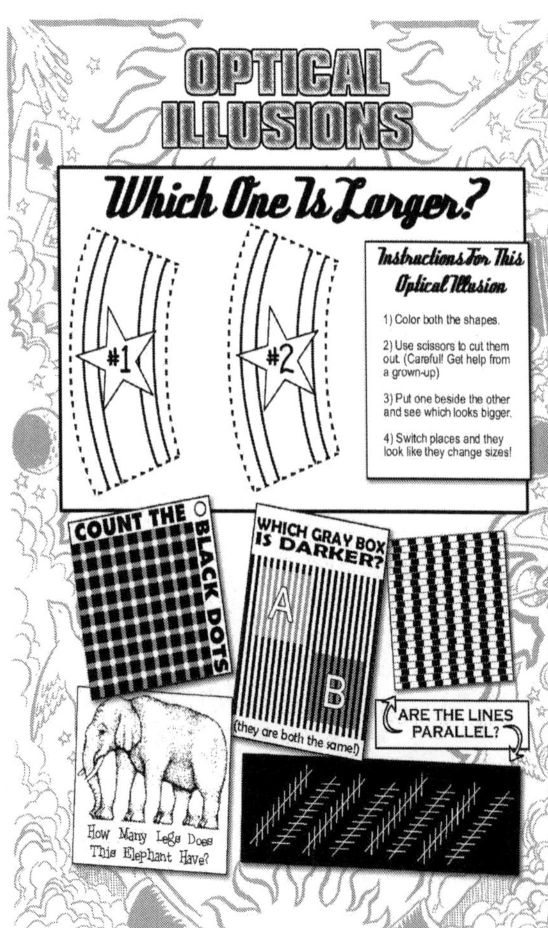
OPTICAL ILLUSIONS
Which One Is Larger?
#1
#2
Instructions For This Optical Illusion
1) Color both the shapes.
2) Use scissors to cut them out. (Careful! Get help from a grown-up)
3) Put one beside the other and see which looks bigger.
4) Switch places and they look like they change sizes!
COUNT THE BLACK DOTS
WHICH GRAY BOX IS DARKER?
A
B
(they are both the same!)
ARE THE LINES PARALLEL?
How Many Legs Does This Elephant Have?

AMAZING MAGIC TRICKS

RUBBER PENCIL

Effect: The magician's solid wand or pencil seems to turn to soft rubber. On command, it turns solid again.

Secret: Hold the wand horizontally in front of you between thumb and forefinger about a third of the way from the end. By moving your hand up and down in short quick moves, the wand will seem to become flexible and appear as if it were made of rubber (see illustration). This is an excellent optical illusion.

Presentation: Tap the wand on something to show that it is solid. Say the magic word and now demonstrate that it is wobbly and flexible. Another magic word and it turns solid again.

QUARTER BACK

Ask your kid brother if he'd like to earn a quarter. Tell him that if he can tear a piece of paper into 4 equal parts, you'll give him a quarter!

He will carefully do so… then demand his quarter! (now, this part is fun!) You hand him one of the 4 pieces of paper, and say, "Here is your quarter." (of the paper)

LAST STRAW

Thread a length of string through a paper straw. Bend the straw- then cut the straw (fig.1). The string will remain unhurt! Follow the directions shown below and you can do this trick!

Secretly cut silt on one side of the straw, in the middle. When you bend the straw, the thread will fall through the slit away from the middle of the straw. When you cut the middle of the straw, the scissors will go above the string.

To finish, pull out the string unharmed, and crumple the straw in the other hand.

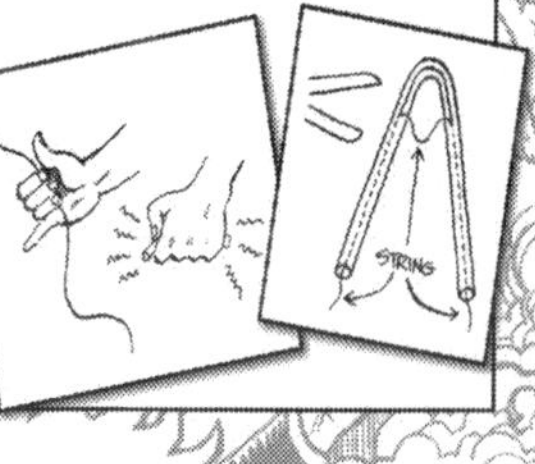

AMAZING (but oh so easy) MAGIC

PENCiL POWER

Effect: The magician makes some mysterious passes around a wand or pencil which uncannily starts to move on its own.

Secret: The magician secretly blows on the wand, which causes it to roll.

Props: Use a wand or pencil, and a smooth table-top.

Preparation: Practice blowing toward the wand gently and secretly.

Presentation: Lay the wand on the table and very slowly trace circles around the outside of the wand with a finger. Then, as you move the finger away, the wand seems to follow. You claim to have created a static field that pulls plastic like a magnet. The trick is that as you draw the finger away from you and from the wand, you blow gently on the wand. The audience is so busy watching the movement of the finger, they won't notice that you are blowing towards the wand, which causes it to roll easily on the flat surface.

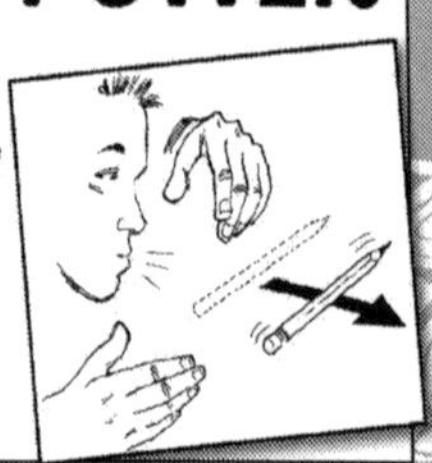

VANiSHiNG RUBBER BANDS

Wrap a rubber band around the tips of both your middle fingers (fig.1). On the edge of a table, show these two fingers (fig.2).

Place both hands under the table edge (fig.3). Then show both index fingers and say, "The rubber bands have disappeared!" (fig.4)

Place both hands under the table again, then show both middle fingers. With a surprised look on your face, declare, "The rubber bands have reappeared!"

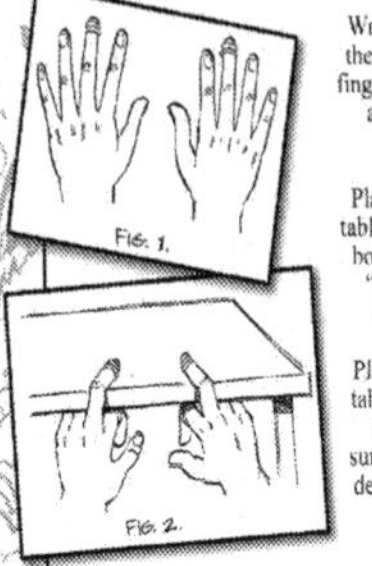

Tricks

Try These Out!

HYPNO-PENCIL

Tell your friends that you can hypnotize an ordinary lead pencil and make it write any color they ask you to!

"Make it write red!" says one. So with a flourish, do just that!

Any other color is just as easy to do!

X-RAY vision

Ask someone to thoroughly shuffle a deck of cards. The cards are handed to you and you put them into the box they came in. You now remove the cards, one by one, but name each card before removing them!

You have, beforehand cut out a little window in the box. This allows you to see the name of the card you are about to show!

RING THING

Tell your pals that you can do an impossible trick!

You say that you can push your whole hand through a finger ring you are holding in your hand!

Of course none of them will believe you! With a big smile, put your finger through the ring and poke your hand. You are 'pushing' your hand through the ring!

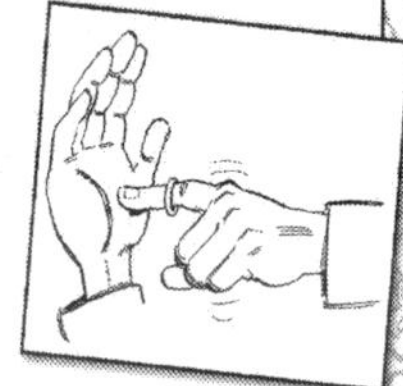

CONTACT INFORMATION:

Share your own personal stories and jokes with Christopher at funnyhypermagicboy.com or by emailing christopherjamescomedy@gmail.com.

Join the Facebook Fan Club: Search for Funny Hyper Magic Boy or go to www.facebook.com/funnyhypermagicboy.

Over 120 Youtube videos online. Visit funnyhypermagicboy.com for the latest links and updates.

Made in the USA
Columbia, SC
16 June 2019